MW01536822

Contents

Publisher's Note		*iv*
Foreword to the Original Edition		*v*
1.	**Introduction**	1
	Significance of name — New meaning introduced into religion	
2.	**Some Distinctive Features of Islam**	3
	Belief in all prophets — Perfection of religion — Unity of mankind — An historical religion	
3.	**The Fundamental Principles of Islam**	6
4.	**The Divine Being**	7
	Conception of God in Islam — Existence of God — Example of Holy Quran — Unity of God	
5.	**Divine Revelation**	12
	Belief in prophets — Perfection of revelation — Continuance of lower forms	
6.	**Life after Death**	16
	is continuation of present life — image of spiritual state in this life — Infinite progress in life after death	
7.	**Significance of Belief**	19
	Belief in angels — Belief as basis for action	
8.	**Principles of Action**	21
9.	**Man's Duties towards God**	22
	Prayer — Fasting — Pilgrimage — Meaningful acts of worship	
10.	**Man's Duties to Man**	26
	Brotherhood of Islam — Rights of women — The State — Illustrations of Islamic rule — Jihād — *Zakāt* and Charity	
11.	**Scope of Moral Teachings**	34

Publisher's Note

Islam — The Religion of Humanity by Maulana Muhammad Ali (d. 1951) was first published in 1928, being a condensed version of the author's introductory Preface in his monumental 1917 publication *The English Translation of the Holy Quran, with Commentary*. This popular booklet ran into numerous reprints, with hundreds of thousands of copies being distributed free all over the world. It was also translated into many languages including French, German, Dutch, Italian, Hungarian, Polish and Chinese.

In view of the popularity of this booklet, it was felt that it should be expanded to give greater details of the noble teachings of Islam. Since its original publication, Maulana Muhammad Ali had produced such highly-acclaimed and invaluable books as *The Religion of Islam* (1936), *The New World Order* (1944), *Living Thoughts of the Holy Prophet Muhammad* (1947), and the revised edition of his *Translation of the Holy Quran with Commentary* (1951). It was also felt that the unique exposition of Islam contained in these books should be made available in a very concise form.

Islam — The Religion of Humanity has, therefore, been enlarged by incorporating suitable passages from the above and other books of the Maulana. While retaining the original form of the booklet, existing sections have been amplified and some new sections added. In making these additions, some minor editing was necessary to ensure continuity and balance in the text.

Such a revised edition was first published in 1980. The present edition contains further revision and addition. The work of revision was conceived and carried out by the Ahmadiyya Anjuman Ishā'at Islam Lahore (U.K. branch), based in Wembley, London, who also did the type-setting and the preparation of the art-work.

Foreword
to the Original Edition

by Lord Headley[1]

With very great pleasure I have read Maulana Muhammad Ali's excellent epitome of Islamic teaching, and I am much impressed by the ability he has shown in condensing, within the space of a few pages, all the essentials of our religion:the simplicity and sincerity of the work cannot but commend it to all those who are earnestly searching for the truth. There is a distinct need of such a concise exposition of Islam, for, notwithstanding the march of education and intelligent reasoning on religious subjects, there still remains in this country a lamentable amount of ignorance respecting the Muslim religion.

To a great extent this is due to the misrepresentations of those who really know, but wilfully mislead the Western mind respecting our faith. Some of the fallacies resulting from this unworthy practice of misrepresentation are that Muslims worship Muhammad, that polygamy is part of the Islamic religion, and that women have no souls. Amazing and incredible as it may seem, I am certain that great many respectable and in other respects fairly educated people in England really believe that we worship Muhammad, are compelled to have great many wives, and that our womenfolk have no souls and cannot enter into Paradise! All these ideas are utterly mistaken. We worship Allah, the one and only God. "Thee only do we worship, and of Thee alone do we beg for assistance," is part of the Muslim prayer, and we

---

1. Lord Headley (d. 1935) was a British peer who embraced Islam in 1913 at the hand of Khwaja Kamal-ud-Din, the pioneer Muslim missionary to Europe, who belonged to the Lahore Ahmadiyya Movement. Lord Headley was closely associated with the Woking Muslim Mission in England, which was founded by Khwaja Kamal-ud-Din and run by members of the Ahmadiyya Anjuman Ishā'at Islam, Lahore.

make no distinction between the prophets selected by the Almighty in various stages of the world's history. There is but one God, and Muhammad is the Prophet, the last Prophet, of God. Polygamy was rampant throughout Arabia before the advent of Muhammad, who merely regulated and placed restrictions on the number of wives a man might have. He also entirely put a stop to female infanticide as practised in Arabia before his time. At the present time, very few Muslims have more than one wife, and woman's position in the Muslim world is far better than it is in Christian countries.

I hope that steps may be taken to have this little work widely distributed, as I feel sure that a perusal of its pages will bring enlightenment and comfort to those who may as yet be unaware of the true spirit of Islam, and may still be labouring under the delusions brought about, either by want of correct information or by listening to those who should know better than to falsely represent a sister religion.

HEADLEY

Islam — The Religion of Humanity

1. INTRODUCTION

Islām is the name by which the religion preached by the Holy Prophet Muhammad, who appeared in Arabia more than thirteen hundred years ago,[1] is known, and it is the last of the great religions of the world. This religion is commonly known in the West as Muhammadanism, a name adopted in imitation of such names as Christianity and Buddhism, but it is quite unknown to the Muslims themselves. According to the Quran, the sacred Book of Islam, the religion of Islam is as wide in its conception as humanity itself. It did not originate from the preaching of the Holy Prophet Muhammad, but it was as well the religion of the prophets that went before him. Islam was the religion of Adam, Noah, Abraham, Moses and Jesus; it was, in fact, the religion of every Prophet of God, who appeared in any part of the world. Nay, Islam is the religion of every human child that is born, according to the Holy Prophet who, to be accurate, is not the originator but the latest exponent of that Divine system which was made perfect at his advent. And according to the Quran, Islam is the natural religion of man:

> "The nature made by God in which He has created man—that is the right religion" (30:30).

And since, according to the Quran, prophets were raised among different nations in different ages, and the religion of every prophet was, in its pristine purity, no other than Islam, the scope of this religion, in the true sense of the word, extends as far back, and is as wide, as humanity itself, the fundamental principles always remaining the same, the accidents changing with the changing needs of humanity. The latest phase of Islam is that which made its appearance in the world with the advent of the Holy Prophet Muhammad — may peace and the blessings of God be upon him!

---

1. Born 571 C.E., died 632 C.E.

Significance of the name

The name *Islām* was not invented, as in the case of other religions, by those who professed it. This name is, on the other hand, expressly given to this religion in the Holy Quran. It says: "I (God) have chosen for you Islam as a religion" (5:3). And in another place: "Surely the religion with God is Islam" (3:18). It is, moreover, a significant name; in fact, the word *Islām* indicates the very essence of the religious system known by that name. Its primary significance is the 'making of peace', and the idea of 'peace' is the dominant idea in *Islām*. A Muslim, according to the Holy Quran, is he who has made peace with God and man, with the Creator as well as His creatures. Peace with God implies complete submission to His will Who is the source of all purity and goodness, and peace with man implies the doing of good to fellow-man. Both these ideas are briefly, but beautifully, expressed in 2:112, which says:

> "Nay, whoever submits himself entirely to God, and is the doer of good to others, he has his reward from his Lord, and there is no fear for such, nor shall they grieve."

That, and that only, is *salvation* according to the Holy Quran. And as the Muslim is in perfect peace, he enjoys peace of mind and contentment (16:106). "Peace" is the greeting of one Muslim to another, and "Peace" shall also be the greeting of those in paradise: "And their greeting therein shall be, Peace" (10:10). Nay, in the paradise which Islam depicts, no word shall be heard except "Peace, Peace", as the Holy Quran says: "They shall hear therein no vain or sinful talk, but only the saying, Peace! Peace!" (56:25,26). The "Author of peace and safety" is also a name of God mentioned in the Holy Quran (59:23), and the goal to which Islam leads is the "Abode of Peace", as is said in 10:25: "And God invites to the abode of peace". Peace is, therefore, the essence of Islam, being the root from which it springs and the fruit which it yields, and Islam is thus pre-eminently the *Religion of Peace*.

New meaning introduced into religion

In Islam the concept of *religion* receives a new significance. Firstly, it is to be treated not as a dogma, which a man must accept if he is to escape everlasting damnation, but as a science based on the universal experience of humanity. Thus, according to Islam, Divine revelation (or God's communicating with man) is a necessary factor in the evolution of man. And from its crudest form (that of true dreams and visions) to its highest form (that of religious truths and laws revealed to the great prophets of God), Divine revelation is the universal experience of humanity and a Divine gift bestowed upon all the nations of the world. Secondly, further strengthening the idea of the scientific in religion, Islam presents all its doctrines as principles of human conduct and action, and makes each point of belief the basis for action by man for his development to higher and yet higher stages of life.

Thirdly, the sphere of religion is not confined to the next world; its primary concern is rather with this life, that man, through a righteous life here on earth, may attain to the consciousness of a higher existence. And so it is that the Quran deals not only with the means which make man attain communion with God, but also with the problems of the world around us, with important questions the proper understanding of which enables man to lead a happy life. It gives guidance for individual progress, and also for the advancement of society, the nation, and even humanity. It prepares man for another life, but only through making him capable of holding his own in the present one.

2. SOME DISTINCTIVE CHARACTERISTICS OF ISLAM

Belief in all the prophets

The great characteristic of Islam is that it requires its followers to believe that all the great religions of the world that prevailed before it were revealed by God; and thus Islam lays down the basis of peace and harmony among the religions of the world. According to the Holy Quran, there is not one nation in the world in which a prophet has not appeared: "There is not a people but a warner has gone among them" (35:24). One is further told that there have been prophets besides those mentioned in the Quran: "And We sent messengers We have mentioned to thee before, and messengers We have not mentioned to thee" (4:164). The Quran, however, not only establishes the theory that prophets have appeared in all nations; it goes further and renders it necessary that a Muslim should believe in all those prophets (2:136, 177, 285), and though the faith of Islam is summed up in two brief sentences, *There is no god but Allah, and Muhammad is His Apostle,* yet the person who confesses belief in Muhammad, in so doing, accepts all the prophets of the world, whether their names are mentioned in the Quran or not. Islam thus claims a universality to which no other religion can aspire, and lays the foundation of a brotherhood as vast as humanity itself.

Perfection of religion
The great mission of Islam was not, however, to preach this truth only, which, on account of the isolation from each other of the different nations of the earth, had not been preached before, but also to correct the errors which had found their way into various religions, to sift truth from error, to preach the truths which had not been preached before on account of the special circumstances of society or the early stage of its development, and most important of all, to gather together in one book the truths which were contained in any Divine revelation granted to any people for the guidance of man; and last of all, to meet all the spiritual and moral requirements of an ever-advancing humanity. Thus Islam claims to be the final and the most perfect expression of the will of God, as the Quran says:

"This day have I perfected for you your religion and completed My favour to you and chosen for you Islam as a religion" (5:3).

Accordingly, the Holy Quran is spoken of as "pure pages, wherein are (all) right books" (98:2,3), the meaning being that all those right directions necessary for the guidance of man, whether previously revealed or not, are to be met with in this Holy Book.

The unity of mankind
According to the Divine scheme whereby prophets were raised for the regeneration of the world, as disclosed in the Quran, every nation had its prophets, and thus, though prophethood was in one sense a universal fact, it was more or less a national institution, the scope of the teaching of every prophet being limited to his own nation. The final

step, therefore, in the institution of prophethood was the coming of one prophet for all the nations, so that the grand idea of unifying the whole human race :ould be brought to perfection. The Holy Prophet Muhammad's mission is thus described in the Holy Quran: "Blessed is God Who sent down the *Furqān* (the Quran) upon His servant that he may be a warner to all the nations" (25:1); and, "Say : O mankind, surely I am the Messenger of God to you all" (7:158). The World-Prophet therefore took the place of the national prophets, all geographical limitations were swept away as were all bars of colour and race, and the basis of the unity of the human race was laid upon the grand principle that "mankind is a single nation" (2:213).

It should be added that such unity of mankind could not be accomplished unless the finality of prophethood was established, for if prophets continued to appear after the World-Prophet they would undoubtedly shatter the very foundations of the unity at which Islam aimed by giving a single prophet to the whole world. Hence it is that the Holy Prophet Muhammad is spoken of as "the Messenger of God and the last of the prophets" (33:40). It may be further added that the object of sending a prophet to a people was to point out the ways by walking in which men could hold communion with God. That object was also brought to perfection through the great World Prophet, whose message was so perfect that it met the requirements not only of all contemporary nations, but of all future generations as well. This is plainly claimed by the Quran (see 5:3 quoted above), a claim not put forward by any other religion. Religion thus being made perfect, there remained no need for another religion after Islam or another prophet after the Prophet Muhammad.

An historical religion
I wish to notice one more peculiarity of Islam by way of introduction. Islam is beyond all doubt an historical religion, and its Holy Founder an historical personage. It is a fact which even an hostile critic of Islam has to admit. Every event of the Holy Prophet's life can be read in the light of history, and the Holy Quran, which is the source of all the spiritual and social laws of Islam, is, as has been remarked by Bosworth

Smith,[1] "a book absolutely unique in its origin, in its preservation . . .
on the substantial authenticity of which no one has ever been able to
cast a serious doubt." Even Muir[2] admits that "there is probably in the
world no other work which has remained twelve centuries with so pure
a text", and adds with Von Hammer that "we hold the Quran to be as
surely Muhammad's word as the Muhammadans hold it to be the word
of God".

Having a book of Divine revelation so safely preserved through
centuries to guide him for his spiritual and moral welfare, and the
example of such a great and noble Prophet whose varied experiences in
life furnish the best rules of conduct in all the different phases of human
life, a Muslim is sure that he has not rejected any truth which was ever
revealed by God to any nation, and that he has not set at naught any
good which was to be found in the life of any good man. A Muslim thus
not only believes in the truth of all Divine revelations and accepts the
sacred leaders of all peoples, but also follows the lasting and permanent
truths contained in those revelations by following the last and most
comprehensive of them, and imitates all good men in all the good that
is to be found in their lives by taking for his model the most perfect
exemplar.

3. THE FUNDAMENTAL PRINCIPLES OF ISLAM

The main principles of Islam are given in the very beginning of the Holy
Quran, which opens with the words:

> "This Book, there is no doubt in it, is a guide to those who keep their duty, who
> believe in the Unseen and keep up prayer and spend (charitably) out of what We
> have given them, and who believe in that which has been revealed to thee (O
> Muhammad) and that which was revealed before thee, and of the Hereafter they
> are sure" (2:2−4).

These verses point out the essential principles which must be accepted
by those who would follow the Holy Quran. Here we have three main

---

1. Author of *Muhammad and Muhammadanism* (London, 1889).

2. Sir William Muir, author of *Life of Muhammad* and other books on Islam, and an
hostile critic of Islam, who lived in the last century.

points of belief and two main points of practice, or three theoretical and two practical ordinances. Before I take up these points separately, I think it necessary to point out, as is indicated in these verses, that in Islam mere belief counts for nothing if not carried into practice. "Those who believe and do good" is the ever-recurring description of the righteous as given in the Quran. Right belief is the good seed which can only grow into a good tree if it receives nourishment from the soil in which it is placed. That nourishment is given by good deeds. Another point necessary to be borne in mind in connection with the five principles of belief and practice mentioned in the verses quoted above is that they are, in one form or another, universally accepted by the human race.

The five principles as already indicated are: (1) a belief in God, the Great Unseen, (2) in Divine revelation, (3) in the life to come; and on the practical side: (4) prayer to God, which is the source from which springs the love of God, and (5) charity in its broadest sense; indicating respectively the performance of our duties to God and man. Now, these five principles of belief and action are recognized by all nations of the earth, and these are the common principles on which all religions are based. In fact, these five fundamental principles of the holy religion of Islam are imprinted on human nature. Here I take them separately as detailed in the Holy Quran.

4. THE DIVINE BEING

Conception of God in Islam

Of the three fundamental principles of belief, the first is a belief in God. The belief in a power higher than man can be traced back to the remotest antiquity, to the earliest times to which history can take us, but different peoples in different ages and different countries have had different conceptions of the Divine Being. Islam, in the first place, preaches a God Who is above all tribal deities and national gods. The God of Islam is not the God of a particular nation, so that He should confine His blessings to it alone, but He is described in the opening words of the Holy Quran to be the "Lord of all the worlds" (1:1), and thus, while giving the highest conception of the Divine Being, it also enlarges the circle of the brotherhood of man so as to include all nations of the earth, thereby widening the outlook and sympathies of man.

Among the numerous sublime attributes of the Divine Being to which the Holy Quran gives expression, the attribute of mercy occupies the highest place. It is with the names *al-Rahmān* and *al-Rahīm* that every chapter of the Holy Book opens. The words *Beneficent* and *Merciful* convey to the English reader of the Holy Quran only a very imperfect idea of the deep and all-encompassing love and mercy of God as indicated by the words *al-Rahmān* and *al-Rahīm*. "My Mercy encompasses all things," says the Holy Quran (7:156). Hence the Messenger who preached this conception of the Divine Being is rightly called in the Holy Quran "a mercy to all the nations" (21:107). Again, God is the Author of all that exists. A denial of His power of creation would have given a death-blow to the very loftiness and sublimity of the conception of the Divine Being. Here is but one description of His attributes:

> "He is Allah besides Whom there is no God, the Knower of the unseen and the seen. He is the Beneficent, the Merciful. He is Allah besides Whom there is no God, the King, the Holy, the Author of peace, the Granter of security, Guardian over all, the Mighty, the Supreme, the Possessor of greatness. Glory be to Allah from that which they set up (as false gods) ! He is Allah, the Creator, the Maker,[1] the Fashioner: His are the most beautiful names. Whatever is in the heavens and the earth declares His glory; and He is the Mighty, the Wise" (59:22 – 24).

God is above all limitations, and He cannot be likened to anything known to man (42:11). While God comprehends all vision, man's vision cannot comprehend Him (6:104). He is One; duality or trinity in Divine nature, or multiplicity of gods, being unthinkable (2:163; 16:51; 4:171); nor does He hold the relation of fatherhood or sonship to anyone (112:3; 19:90 – 93). He is Omniscient (20:7), Omnipotent (16:48 – 50), and Omnipresent (58:7), being nearer to man than his own self (50:16; 56:85). There is a very large number of other attributes of

---

1. The original word for *Maker* is *Bārī,* which signifies especially the Maker of souls as distinct from the Creator of matter.

the Divine Being which give a loftiness to the conception of God in the Quran not met with in any other revealed book.

The Existence of God

Faith in God being the foundation of Islam, three kinds of arguments are advanced relating to the existence of God:

1.   Evidence is drawn from the material universe that there must be a Creator and Controller of the universe. In the Holy Quran, this evidence centres around the word *Rabb,* the first attribute of the Divine Being to which Revelation draws attention—"Read in the name of thy *Rabb*" (96:1)—and with which the Holy Quran begins (1:1), being also the oftest repeated attribute in the Holy Book. *Rabb,* usually translated as *Lord* for the sake of brevity, means *the Fosterer of a thing in such a manner as to make it attain one condition after another until it reaches its goal of perfection.* Everything created thus bears the impress of Divine creation in the characteristic of moving on from lower to higher stages until it reaches completion. Evolution, which has proved a stumbling block to other religions, is thus made in Islam the very basis of belief in God, and serves as an argument of purpose and wisdom in creation. The oneness of law prevailing in the universe, notwithstanding the immensity of its diversity (67:3,4), existence of the strictest control throughout Nature from the tiniest particle to the mightiest sphere (36:38; 55:5,6), and similar other arguments run through every page of the Holy Book.

2.   The second group of arguments for the existence of God relates to the human soul in which is implanted, according to the Holy Quran, the consciousness of Divine existence. An appeal is again and again made to man's inner self: "Were they created for nothing?" "Are they creators of their own souls?" "Did they create the heavens and the earth?" (52:35,36). "Am I not your *Rabb*?" (7:172). God-consciousness is thus shown to be part and parcel of human nature. Sometimes this consciousness is mentioned in terms of the unimaginable nearness of the human spirit to the Divine Spirit: "We are nearer to man than his life-vein" (50:16); "We are nearer to your soul than you" (56:85). This is to show that the consciousness of the existence of God in the human soul is even clearer than the consciousness of its own existence. This

consciousness undoubtedly differs in different natures according as the inner light of man is bright or dim.

This argument is further strengthened by showing that there is something more than mere consciousness of the existence of God. The spirit of God has been breathed into man (15:29), and hence it is that the soul of man yearns after God; there is in it the instinct to serve God and to turn to Him for help (1:4). Every man, even the polytheist, turns to God in affliction and distress, when the full strength of human nature asserts itself (10:12,22; 39:8). There is, further, implanted in man faith in God, by which he is guided through darkness and difficulty (10:9); love of God, out of which selfless service is rendered to humanity (2:177; 76:8); trust in God, which is an unfailing source of strength to man in times of failure (14:12).

3.   The surest and clearest evidence of the existence of God is, however, afforded by the spiritual—the higher—experience of humanity, by God revealing Himself to man. The evidence of wisdom and purpose in the universe only shows that there *must be* a God, and does not lead to the certain conviction that God *is;* the evidence of the inner self of man is also insufficient to lead to this certain conviction and give man access to the Divine Being; it is Divine revelation that not only establishes the greatest reality of this life that God *is,* but also casts a flood of light on the Divine attributes and sets man on the way by walking in which he feels His existence as a reality in his own life and which enables him to hold communion with Him. It is this realization of the Divine Being that works a change in man's life and gives him an irresistible spiritual force through which he can bring about a change even in others' lives. God's revealing Himself to man is, according to Islam, the universal experience of humanity, the experience of men in all nations, all countries and all ages. It is this universal spiritual experience of mankind that has proved a force of the first magnitude in lifting up humanity from the depths of degradation to the greatest heights of moral and even material advancement.

Example of the Holy Quran
The Holy Quran provides the greatest example of the existence and working of God being shown through Divine revelation. It discloses

sublime truths and principles which could not have been the human knowledge of an unlettered Arab living in the seventh century, as was the Holy Prophet Muhammad. It brought about a transformation unparalleled in the history of the world. In no more than twenty-three years (609 – 632 C.E.) a complete change was wrought in the lives of the whole nation inhabiting the Arabian peninsula, a land where centuries of previous reformation work had proved fruitless. Deep-rooted idol-worship was replaced by the worship of one God; all superstitions were swept away and in their place came the most rational religion the world could imagine; the people who prided themselves on ignorance became the greatest lovers of knowledge, drinking deep at every fountain of learning to which they could get access; oppression of the weak, the poor, the slaves and women, gave place to justice and equality; and a nation steeped in the deepest vices was thoroughly purified and became charged with a burning desire for the noblest deeds in the service of humanity. The Quran accomplished a transformation not just of the individual, but equally of the family, of society, of an entire nation, and, through that nation, of humanity itself. There is no other book which has brought about a change so miraculous in the lives of men, raising them from the depths of degradation to the highest pinnacle of civilization.

The Holy Quran not only produced this grand transformation, but from the very start of the Holy Prophet's career it announced prophecy after prophecy, in the surest and most certain terms, to the effect that the implacable opposition would perish and Islam would be triumphant. These prophecies were declared at a time when the Holy Prophet was quite alone and helpless, beset on all sides by fierce opposition, and there was not the remotest prospect of Islam ever making any headway. Yet they were fulfilled only a. few years afterwards in an astounding manner. No man could possibly have foreseen what was so clearly foretold as certain to come about, and no human power could have brought to utter failure a whole nation ranged against a solitary man. Divine revelation thus affords the clearest and surest proof of the existence of God, Whose infinite knowledge comprehends the future as well as the past and present, and Who controls both the forces of nature and the destiny of man.

The Unity of God

Unity of God is the one great theme of the Holy Quran. Its best-known expression is that contained in the declaration of *lā ilāha ill-Allāh* ("there is no god but Allah"), which conveys the significance that there is nothing which deserves to be worshipped except Allah. The Unity of God means, firstly, that there is neither plurality of gods nor plurality of persons in the Godhead, secondly that no other being possesses any Divine attribute in perfection, and thirdly that none can do that which God has done, or which God may do.

The opposite of Unity is *shirk* (the associating of 'gods' with God, or ascribing Divine qualities to others than God), which is said to be the gravest of all sins (31:13) due to the fact that it demoralizes man, while Divine Unity brings about his moral elevation. The various forms of *shirk* mentioned in the Quran include: worship of things such as idols, animals, forces of nature, etc., supposing other things and beings to possess the same attributes as God, as in the doctrine of trinity or of the co-eternity of matter and soul, blindly following the behests of great men, and blind submission to one's own desires. These show that, in the doctrine of Unity, the Quran gives to the world an ennobling message of advancement all round, physical as well as moral and spiritual. Man is freed not only from slavery to animate and inanimate objects, but also from subservience to the wonderous forces of nature which, he is told, he can subdue for his own benefit (45:12,13). It goes further and delivers man from that greatest of slaveries—slavery to man. It does not allow to any mortal the dignity of Godhead, or of being more than a mortal; for the greatest of mortals (the Holy Prophet) is commanded to say: "I am only a mortal like you; it is revealed to me that your God is One God" (18:110). Thus all the bonds which fettered the mind of man were broken, and he was set on the road to progress.

5. DIVINE REVELATION

The second fundamental principle of faith in the Islamic religion is belief in the Divine revelation, not only a belief in the truth of the revealed Word of God as found in the Holy Quran, but a belief in the truth of Divine revelation in all ages and to all nations of the earth. Divine revelation is the basis of all revealed religions, but the principle is accepted subject to various limitations. Some religions consider revelation to have been granted to mankind only once; others look upon it as limited to a particular people; while still others close the door of revelation after a certain time. With the advent of Islam, we find the same breadth of view introduced into the conception of the Divine revelation as in the conception of the Divine Being.

According to the Holy Quran, revelation in its lower forms, in the form of inspiration or that of dreams and visions, is the universal experience of humanity. Similarly, in its highest form, that of Divinely-revealed scriptures and laws, it is not limited to one particular man or to one particular nation, but has been granted to each and every nation. Without the assistance of revelation from God, no people could have ever attained the communion with God, and hence it was necessary that Almighty God, Who, being the Lord of the whole world, supplied all men with their physical necessities, should also have brought to them His spiritual blessings. Thus the idea of revelation in Islam is as broad as humanity itself, and a Muslim is required to believe, not in the Quran alone, but in all the Books of God, granted to all the nations of the world.

Belief in the Prophets
As the revelation of a Book of God must be communicated through a man, faith in the messenger is a natural sequence, and is mentioned in the Quran along with faith in the revealed books. The prophet is not only the bearer of the Divine message, but he also shows how that message is to be interpreted in practical life; and therefore he is the model to be followed. It is his example that inspires a living faith in the hearts of his followers and brings about a real transformation in their lives. Hence there is a deeper significance underlying faith in the prophets. As stated earlier (see Section 2), a belief in all the prophets of the world is an essential principle of the religion of Islam. The Holy Quran has plainly said that prophets appeared in all nations and that it has not named all of them, which in fact was unnecessary. Therefore, a Muslim may accept the great luminaries of old venerated by any other

nation as having brought it light and guidance, as the prophets of that nation.

Perfection of Revelation

According to the teachings of Islam, revelation is not only universal but also progressive, attaining perfection in the last of the Prophets, the Holy Prophet Muhammad. A revelation was granted to each nation according to its requirements, and in each age in accordance with the capacity of the people of that age. And as the human brain became more and more developed, more and yet more light was cast by revelation on matters such as the existence and attributes of God, the nature of revelation from Him, the requital of good and evil, the life after death, and so on. The Quran, the final revealed scripture, shed complete light on all the essentials of religion, made manifest what had hitherto remained, of necessity, obscure, and brought religion to perfection.

Besides this, the Quran points out that the teachings of earlier scriptures had undergone alterations, and therefore only a revelation from God could separate the pure Divine teaching from the mass of error which had grown around it. This the Quran did, and hence it is called a "guardian" over the earlier scriptures. It also claims to be a judge, deciding the differences between them. All religions were from God, but even their basic doctrines had come to differ from one another to such an extent that it had become simply unthinkable that they could have proceeded from the same Divine source; till the Quran pointed out the common ground, namely, the Unity of God, and the universality of revelation.

Continuance of lower forms of revelation

Islam not only makes Divine revelation the universal experience of humanity, but also considers its door as standing open for all time. Though revelation was made perfect and prophethood came to a close in the person of the Holy Prophet Muhammad, God still speaks to His elect among the Muslims. Revelation in its lower forms—in the form of true dreams, visions and inspiration—is common to both prophets and those who are not prophets.[1] It is only authoritative revelation, the form of revelation peculiar to prophets, that has ceased after the Holy Prophet Muhammad. Thus he is reported to have said: "Nothing remains of prophethood except *mubashshirāt*"; and being asked what was meant by *mubashshirāt*, he replied, "True visions". We are told in another of his Sayings:

"Among the nations before you, there used to be persons who were spoken to by God though they were not prophets; if there is such a one among my people, it is Umar."

This shows that, though there are to be no prophets after the Holy Prophet Muhammad, religion and religious laws having been made perfect at his advent, Divine revelation is still a fact and a true Muslim can have access to it. It is through His word that real conviction comes to the heart that God exists, and it is through the elect who receive His revelation that a vital faith in God is restored.

There is also another aspect of the Islamic belief in Divine revelation in which it differs from some other religions of the world. It refuses to acknowledge the incarnation of the Divine Being. That the highest aim of religion is communion with God is a fact universally recognized. According to the Holy Quran, this communion is not attained by God assuming a human shape in the sense of incarnation, but by man rising gradually towards God by spiritual progress and the purification of his life from all sensual desires and low motives. The perfect one who reveals the face of God to the world is not the Divine Being in human form, but the human being whose person has become a manifestation of the Divine attributes by his own personality having been consumed in the fire of love for God. His example serves as incentive and is a model for others to follow. He shows by his example how a mortal can attain to communion with God. Hence the broad principle of Islam that no one is precluded from being fed from the source of Divine revelation, and that anyone can attain it by following the Holy Word of God as revealed in the Holy Quran.

---

1. See the Quran, 28:7, 5:111 etc.

6. LIFE AFTER DEATH

Belief in a future life, in one form or another, is also common to all religions of the world, and it is the third fundamental article of a Muslim's faith. The mystery of the life after death has, however, nowhere been solved so clearly as in Islam. The idea of a life after death was so obscure till as late as the appearance of the Jewish religion, that not only is there not much of it found in the Old Testament but an important Jewish sect actually denied any such state of existence. This was, however, due to the fact that much light was not thrown upon it in earlier revelation. The belief in transmigration (or reincarnation of souls) was also due to the undeveloped mind of man mistaking spiritual realities for physical facts. In Islam, the idea reached its perfection, as did other important fundamental principles of religion. Belief in a future life implies the accountability of man in another life for actions done in this. The belief is no doubt a most valuable basis for the moral elevation of the world, if properly understood. The following points are particularly emphasized by the Holy Quran.

Life after death is only a continuation of the life below
The gulf that is generally interposed between this life and the life after death is the great obstacle in the solution of the mystery of the hereafter. Islam makes that gulf disappear altogether: it makes the next life as only a continuation of the present life. On this point the Holy Quran is explicit. It says:

> "We have (in this very life) made the consequences of a man's deeds cling to his neck, and these hidden consequences We will bring to light on the Day of Resurrection in the form of a book wide open" (17:13,14).

And again it says:

> "Whoever is blind in this life, he will be blind in the hereafter; nay, straying further away from the path" (17:72).

And elsewhere we have:

> "O soul that art at rest! return to thy Lord, He being pleased with thee and thou being pleased with Him. So enter among My servants and enter My Garden" (89:27 – 30).

The first of these quotations makes it clear that the great facts which shall be brought to light on the day of Resurrection shall not be anything new, but only a manifestation of what is hidden from the physical eye here. The life after death is, therefore, not a new life, but only a continuation of this life, bringing its hidden realities to light. The other two quotations show that a hellish and a heavenly life both begin in this world. The blindness of the next life is hell, but according to the verse quoted only those who are blind here shall be blind hereafter, thus making it clear that the spiritual blindness of this life is the real hell, and from here it is carried along to the next life. Similarly, it is the soul that has found perfect peace and rest that is made to enter into paradise at death, thus showing that the paradise of the next life is only a continuation of the peace and rest which a man enjoys spiritually in this life. Thus it is clear that, according to the Holy Quran, the next life is a continuation of this, and death is not an interruption but a connecting link, a door that opens up the hidden realities of this life.

State after death is an image of the spiritual state in this life
With Islam, the most significant truth with regard to the next life has been brought to light. In the Christian teaching the corporeal and the spiritual are melted together, weeping and wailing and gnashing of teeth and the quenchless fire as the punishment of the wicked are spoken of in the same breath with the kingdom of heaven, the treasure in heaven and the life eternal as the reward of the righteous; but there is no clear indication as to the sources of the one or the other. The Holy Quran, on the other hand, makes it clear that the state after death is a complete representation, a full and clear image, of our spiritual state in this life. Here the good or bad conditions of the deeds or beliefs of a man are latent within him, and their poison or panacea casts its influence upon him only secretly, but in the life to come they shall become manifest and clear as daylight. The shape which our deeds and their consequences assume in this very life is not visible to the eye of man in this life, but in the next life it will be unrolled in all its clearness. The pleasures and pains of the next life, therefore, though spiritual in reality, will not be hidden from the ordinary eye as spiritual facts are in this life. It is for this reason that while, on the one hand, the blessings of the next life are mentioned by physical names as an evidence of their

clear representation to the eye, they are on the other hand spoken of as things which "the eye has not seen, nor has the ear heard, nor has it entered into the heart of man to conceive of them". This description of the blessings of the next life is really an explanation given by the Holy Prophet himself of the verse of the Quran which says that no soul knows the blessings and joys which have been kept secret for it (32:17).

The following verse of the Holy Quran, which may ordinarily be misunderstood, is far from describing the heavenly blessings as being identical with the things of this world. It runs thus:

> "And give good news to those who believe and do good deeds, that for them are gardens in which rivers flow. Whenever they are given a portion of the fruits thereof, they shall say, 'This is what was given to us before,' and they are given the like of it" (2:25).

Now the fruits which the righteous are made to speak of as having tasted in this life could not possibly be the fruits of trees or the things of this life. The verse, in fact, tells us that those who believe and do good deeds prepare a paradise with their own hands for themselves, with their good deeds for fruits. It is of the fruits of this garden that they are spiritually made to taste here, and of the same, only in a more palpable form, shall they eat in the next life. To the same effect we may quote another verse of the Holy Quran: "On that day you will see the faithful men and the faithful women, their light gleaming before them and on their right hand" (57:12). This verse shows that the light of faith by which the righteous men and women were guided in this life, and which could be seen here only with the spiritual eye, shall be clearly seen going before the believers on the day of Resurrection.

As in the case of the blessings of paradise, the punishment of hell is also an image of the spiritual tortures of this life. Hell is said to be a place where one shall neither live nor die (20:74). It should be remembered in this connection that the Quran describes those who walk in error and wickedness as dead and lifeless, while the good it calls living. The secret of this is that the means of the life of those who are ignorant of God, being simply eating and drinking and the satisfaction of physical desires, are entirely cut off at their death. Of spiritual food they have no share, and therefore, while devoid of true life, they shall be raised again to taste of the evil consequences of their evil deeds.

Infinite progress in life after death

Islam teaches that man is destined to make infinite progress in the life after death. Underlying this is the principle that the development of man's faculties as it takes place in this life is not sealed by finality; but a much wider vista of progress opens out after death. Hell is meant only to purify a man of the dross which he has accumulated with his own hands, in order to make him fit for spiritual advancement in that life. Verses 106 and 107 of the 11th chapter of the Quran show clearly that the punishment of hell is not everlasting. There are also Sayings of the Holy Prophet and his Companions which leave little doubt that hell is a temporary place for the sinner, whether Muslim or non-Muslim, and that the chastisement of hell is a remedy to heal his spiritual diseases and to enable him to start again on the road to the higher life. Nor is paradise a place for simple enjoyment; it is essentially a place for advancement to higher and higher stages (39:20). Those in paradise are spoken of as having an unceasing desire for attaining to higher and higher excellences, their prayer therein being: "Our Lord, make perfect for us our light" (66:8).

7. SIGNIFICANCE OF BELIEF

Belief in angels and its significance

I have now briefly indicated the three fundamental principles of a Muslim's faith, but I may further add that belief in the "unseen" also includes a belief in those agencies which we call angels. This belief, though common to many religions, is not as widely accepted as the three principles explained above, and therefore a few remarks relating to the truth underlying this belief will not be out of place here. In the physical world we find it as established law that we stand in need of external agents, notwithstanding the faculties and powers within us. The eye has been given to us to see things, and it does see them, but not without the help of external light. The ear receives the sound, but independently of the agency of air it cannot serve that purpose. Man, therefore, essentially stands in need of something besides what is within him, and as in the physical, so also in the spiritual world.

Just as our physical faculties are not by themselves sufficient to enable us to attain any object in the physical world without the assistance of other agents, so our own spiritual powers cannot by themselves lead us to do good or evil deeds; but here too, intermediaries which have an existence independent of our internal spiritual powers are necessary to enable us to do good or evil deeds. In other words, there are two attractions placed in the nature of man: the attraction to good or to rise up to higher spheres of virtue, and the attraction to evil, or to stoop down to a kind of low, bestial life; but to bring these attractions into operation external agencies are needed, as they are needed in the case of the physical powers of man. The external agency which brings the attraction to good into work is called an *angel,* and that which assists in the working of the attraction to evil is called the *devil.* If we respond to the attraction for good, we are following the Holy Spirit, and if we respond to the attraction for evil, we are following the Satan. The real significance of belief in angels is, therefore, that we should follow the inviter to good or the attraction for good which is placed within us.

Belief as basis for action
The above remarks explain not only the significance of a Muslim's belief in angels, but also the meaning underlying the very word *belief.* Belief, according to Islam, is not only a conviction of the truth of a given proposition, but it is essentially the acceptance of a proposition as the basis for action. As already shown, the proposition of the existence of the devils is as true as that of the existence of the angels; but while belief in angels is again and again mentioned as part of a Muslim's faith, nowhere are we required to believe in the devils. Both facts are equally true, and the Holy Quran speaks on numerous occasions of the misleadings and insinuations of the devils, but while it requires belief in the angels, it does not require belief in the devils. If belief in angels were only an equivalent to an admission of their existence, belief in devils was an equal necessity. But it is not so. The reason is that whereas man is required to accept and follow the call of the inviter to good, he is required not to follow the call of the inviter to evil, and therefore, as the former gives a basis for action which the

latter does not, we believe in the angels but not in the devils. On the other hand, the Holy Quran requires *disbelief* in the devils: "So whoever disbelieves in the devil and believes in God, he indeed lays hold on the firmest handle" (2:256).

It can thus be seen that the principles of belief enumerated above, as given in the Holy Quran, are really principles each of which serves as the basis for action, and no other belief is known to Islam. The word *Allāh*—the Arabic word for God—indicates that Being Who possesses all the perfect attributes, and when a Muslim is required to believe in Allah, he is really required to make himself the possessor of all those attributes of perfection. The belief in Divine revelation makes him accept and imitate all the good that is met with in the lives of righteous men, and the belief in the hereafter is equivalent to the recognition of the principle of accountability for one's actions.

8. PRINCIPLES OF ACTION

Next we take the practical side of the faith of Islam. As I have already said, in Islam actions are essentially a component part of religion as belief. In this respect Islam occupies a middle position between religions which have ignored the practical side altogether and those which bind their followers to a very minute ritual. It sees the necessity of developing the faculties of man by giving general directions, and then leaves ample scope for the individual to exercise his judiciousness.

Without a strong practical character any religion is likely to pass into mere idealism, and it will cease to exercise influence on the practical life of man. The precepts of Islam, which inculcate duties towards God and duties towards man, are based on that deep knowledge of the human nature which cannot be possessed but by the Author of that nature. They cover the whole range of the development of man, and are thus wonderfully adapted to the requirements of different peoples. In the Holy Quran are found guiding rules for the ordinary man of the world as well as the philosopher, and for communities in the lower grade of civilization as well as the most highly civilized nations of the world. Practicality is the keynote of its precepts, and thus the same

universality which marks its principles of faith is met with in its
practical ordinances, suiting as they do the requirements of all ages and
nations.

9. MAN'S DUTIES TOWARDS GOD

Prayer
The verses of the Holy Quran quoted earlier (see Section 3) form, as I
have already said, the nucleus of the teachings of Islam. Taken in the
broadest sense, the two principles of action mentioned in these verses
stand for the fulfilment of man's duties towards God and his duties
towards man.[1] Prayer to God is the essence of man's duties towards
God. It is an outpouring of the heart's sentiments, a devout
supplication to God, and a reverential expression of the soul's sincerest
desires before its Maker. In Islam the idea of prayer, like all other
religious ideas, finds its highest development. Prayer, according to the
Holy Quran, is the true means of that purification of the heart which is
the only way to communion with God. The Holy Quran says:

> "Recite that which has been revealed to you of the Book, and keep up prayer.
> Surely prayer keeps one away from indecency and evil; and certainly the
> remembrance of God is the greatest (force)" (29:45).

Islam, therefore, enjoins prayer as a means of the moral elevation of
man. Prayer degenerating into mere ritual, into a lifeless and vapid
ceremony gone through with insincerity of heart, is not the prayer
enjoined by Islam. Such prayer is expressly denounced: "Woe to the
praying ones! who are unmindful of their prayers, who do good to be
seen" (107:4 – 6). It is also stated in the same passage that prayer is
useless unless it leads to the service of humanity.

In Islam there is no Sabbath or a day of the week set apart for
worship. Prayer is made a part of the everyday affairs of man. It is the
first daily act of a Muslim and it is also his last one, and between these
two there are three other prayers during hours of business or
recreation. Thus Islam requires that, even when busiest, a Muslim

---

1. ". . . those who . . . keep up prayer and spend (charitably) out of what We have
given them."

should still be able to disengage himself from all worldly occupations for a short while and resort to prayer. Hence it is also that Islam has done away with all institutions of monkery, which require a man to give up all worldly occupations for the whole of his life in order to hold communion with God. Islam makes communion with God possible even when man is most busy with his worldly occupations, thus making possible what was considered impossible before its advent.

The Islamic mode of worship is calculated to concentrate attention on one object: the realization of the Divine presence. The ablution preceding prayer, the reverential attitude in standing, the bowing down, the prostration and the reverent sitting posture—all help the mind to realize the Divine presence as a fact; and the worshipper finds his heart's joy in doing honour to the Great Master, not only with his tongue but with his whole body.

In Islam, the daily congregational prayers are also the means of levelling all differences of rank, colour and nationality, and the means of bringing about a cohesion and unity among people which is the necessary basis of a lasting civilization. Before their Maker, all the worshippers stand shoulder to shoulder, the ruler along with his humblest subject, the rich with the beggar, the white man with the black. Nay, the king or the rich man in a back row will have to lay his head, while prostrating himself before God, at the feet of a poor man in the front. Differences of rank, wealth and colour vanish within the mosque, and an atmosphere of brotherhood, equality and love prevails within its precincts. In fact, the five daily prayers are meant, among other things, to carry into practice the theoretical lessons of equality and fraternity for which Islam stands.

But while Islam has given permanence to the institution of prayer by requiring its observance at stated times and in a particular manner, it has also left ample scope for the individual himself, particularly in the private portion of the prayer, to make any supplications that he likes and in any language that he chooses, in any of the four postures (standing, bowing, prostrating or sitting).

Fasting

Fasting is one of those religious institutions which, though universally recognized, have had quite a new meaning introduced into them by Islam. It rejected totally the idea of appeasing Divine wrath, or exciting Divine compassion through voluntary suffering, and introduced in its place regular fasting as a spiritual, moral and physical discipline of the highest order. The object of this institution is clearly stated in the Holy Quran: "Fasting is prescribed for you . . . so that you may guard against evil" (2:183).

Islam has set apart the month of *Ramadaan* for this purpose. Every day in this month, one is required to abstain from food and drink and sexual intercourse from dawn till sunset. But fasting also means refraining from every kind of evil. In fact, abstention from food is only a step to make a man realize that if he can, in obedience to God, abstain from that which is otherwise lawful, how much more necessary it is that he should abstain from the evil ways which are forbidden by God!

No temptation is greater than the temptation of satisfying one's thirst and hunger when food and drink are in one's possession, yet this temptation is overcome by the faster, not once or twice, as if it were by chance, but day after day regularly for a whole month, with a set purpose of drawing closer and closer to God. Whenever a temptation comes before him, he overcomes it because there is an inner voice, "God is with me," "God sees me"; so the Divine presence becomes a reality for him, and a new consciousness of a higher life—a life above that which is maintained by eating and drinking—is awakened in him, and this is the life spiritual.

Pilgrimage (*Ḥajj*)

The Pilgrimage to Makka, the performance of which is incumbent upon every Muslim once in his life if he has the means, represents the last stage in the progress of the spiritual pilgrim. It represents the stage in which man completely surrenders himself to the Divine will, and sacrifices all his interests and discards all his comforts of life for the love of God. The first requirement of the Pilgrimage, known as *Ihrām*, in which all costly dresses are cast off and the pilgrim has only two seamless wrappers to cover himself, represents the severance of all worldly connections for the love of God. Another prominent feature of the Pilgrimage is *Ṭawāf*, the circumambulation of the Ka'ba,[1] and by performing this external act the pilgrim shows that the fire of Divine love has been kindled within his heart, and like the true lover, he makes circuits around the House of his beloved One. In fact, the whole condition of the pilgrim and all the different devotions connected with the Pilgrimage represent the stage in which the worshipper, imbued with true love of the Divine Being, shows that he has completely surrendered himself to his beloved Master and sacrificed all his interests for His sake.

At the annual occasion of the Pilgrimage, there is a unique assemblage of humanity at Makka, hundreds of thousands of people all inspired by the one idea of feeling the presence of the Divine Being, all concentrating their minds on the One Supreme Being Who for the time is their sole object. Added to this is the mighty effect of the outward unity of them all, clad in the same two sheets, crying out in one language what is understood by all: *lubbaika Allahumma lubbaika* – "Here we are, O Allah! here we are in Thy presence". God is surely not in Makka to the exclusion of other places, yet that vast assemblage feels His presence as if He were actually there in their very midst. Such is the higher spiritual experience of the pilgrims, the experience not of the hermit shut up in his closet, but the experience of a mighty concourse gathered together in one place.

The Pilgrimage also has a wonderful influence, like no other institution in the world, in levelling all distinctions of race, colour, nation, rank or wealth. Not only do people of all races and all countries meet together as God's servants, but there is nothing to distinguish the high from the low. There is a vast concourse of human beings, all clad in one dress, all moving in one way, all having but one word to speak. Thus is every Muslim made to pass once in his life through that narrow gate of equality that leads to broad brotherhood. All men are equal in

---

1. The *Ka'ba* is the simple, rectangular building which has stood as a Divine shrine in Makka from very remote antiquity. It should be noted that Muslims do not worship the Ka'ba, which is, in fact, a memorial to the belief in the oneness of God.

birth and death, but the Pilgrimage is the only occasion on which they are taught how to live alike, how to act alike and how to feel alike.

Meaningful and practicable acts of worship
It would thus be seen that all these Islamic precepts are only meant for the moral elevation of man. Islam does not lay down any institution which may be said to be a meaningless worship of God. The aim and object of all the precepts it gives is the purification of the heart, so that thus purified, man may enjoy communion with the Holy One Who is the Fountain-head of all purity. It would also be seen that Islam introduces workable ascetic formulae into the daily life of man. The five daily prayers require the sacrifice of a small part of his time and, without interfering with his everyday life, enable him to realize the Divine that is within him. Fasting requires the giving up of food and drink, but not in such a manner as to make him unfit for carrying on his regular work. The Pilgrimage is a function which one performs generally only once in a lifetime, and therefore, while leading a man through the highest spiritual experience, it does not interfere in any appreciable degree with the regular course of his life.

10. MAN'S DUTIES TO MAN

The second branch of the Islamic precepts relates to man's duties towards man, but it should be borne in mind that both kinds of precepts are very closely inter-related. The moral elevation of man is the grand theme of the Holy Quran and the chief object which Islam has in view throughout, and all its precepts are only meant to raise humanity step by step to the highest moral elevation to which man can attain. "The person who violates his brother's right is not a believer in the Unity of God"[1] is a teaching which deserves to be written in letters of gold.

The Brotherhood of Islam
In the first place, Islam abolishes all invidious distinctions. "Surely the noblest among you in the sight of God is he who is the most righteous

---

1. A Saying of the Holy Prophet Muhammad.

of you" sounds the death-knell of all superiority or inferiority based on rigid caste and social distinctions. Mankind is but one family according to the Holy Quran which says:

> "O mankind! Surely We have created you from a male and a female and made you tribes and families that you may know each other. Surely the noblest among you in the sight of God is he who is the most righteous of you" (49:13).

Islam thus lays down the basis of a vast brotherhood in which all men and women, to whatever tribe or nation or caste they may belong, and whatever be their profession or rank in society, the wealthy and the poor, have equal rights, and in which no one can trample upon the rights of his brother. In this brotherhood all members should treat each other as members of the same family. No one is to be deprived of any right on the score of his race or profession or sex. Besides being the only religion which enjoined the duty of freeing slaves, and the only religion whose Founder set a personal example of obtaining freedom for slaves, Islam also required a slave to be clothed with the clothing and fed with the food of his master, and not to be treated as a low or vile person. And this great brotherhood did not remain a brotherhood in theory, but became an actual living force by the noble example of the Holy Prophet and his worthy successors and companions. The strict rule of brotherhood is laid down in the following words of the Holy Prophet: "No one of you is a believer in God until he loves for his brother what he loves for himself".

Rights of women

No other religious book and no other reformer, religious or secular, has done one-tenth of what the Holy Quran or the Holy Prophet Muhammad has done to raise the position of women. From a matcrial as well as a spiritual point of view, Islam recognizes the position of woman to be the same as that of man. The highest favour which God has bestowed upon mankind is the gift of Divine revelation, and we find women, as well as men, spoken of in the Quran as receiving revelation (see, for example, 3:41 and 28:7). The Quran makes no difference between man and woman in the bestowal of Divine reward for good deeds:

"Whoever does good, whether male or female, and is a believer, these shall enter
the Garden (of heaven)" (40:40; see also 3:194, 4:124, 16:97 and 33:35).

Thus, according to the clearest teachings of Islam, men and women can
rise to the same eminence in the moral and spiritual spheres.

On the material side too, woman is recognized as on a par with man.
She can earn money and own property just as a man can do: "For men
is the benefit of what they earn, and for women is the benefit of what
they earn" (4:32). She has full control over her property and can
dispose of it as she likes. In Arabia, at the time of the advent of the Holy
Prophet, a woman had no rights of property; in fact, she herself was
part of the inheritance, and was taken possession of along with other
property. The Quran took her from this low position and raised her to
a position of perfect freedom as regards her property rights and her
right to inheritance, a position which, even in modern western nations,
she has attained only very recently after a long struggle.

To raise the moral status of society, Islam requires both sexes to
behave modestly and to develop the habit of keeping their looks cast
down in the presence of each other. When going out, or on other
occasions when there is intermingling of the sexes, women are required
to be properly dressed,[1] and not to make a display of beauty so as to
excite the passions of the other sex. With these precautions, women
have every liberty to go anywhere and to do any work.

As a wife, a woman does not lose any of the rights she possesses as an
individual member of society; nor is her individuality merged in that of
her husband. Her position as wife, according to a Saying of the Holy
Prophet, is that of "a ruler over the house of her husband". In the
matter of divorce too, which may become necessary if all means to
effect reconciliation between husband and wife are exhausted, the
Quran places the two parties on a level of perfect equality.

---

1. There is no injunction in Islam requiring women to wear a veil. In the Holy
Prophet's time, women joined the prayers in the mosque without a veil, and the only
separation was that they stood in separate rows behind those of the men. In the
Pilgrimage, women were actually forbidden to wear a veil, as it was a mark of high
rank.

The State

The Holy Prophet Muhammad was not only the Founder of a religion but also the Founder of a state. Like the religion he founded, his ideal for a state was democratic, but it was a democracy based upon responsibility to God in the first place. The following description of believers shows how these two ideas of democratizing and spiritualizing the state were blended:

> "And those who respond to their Lord and keep up prayer, and whose affairs are (decided) by counsel among themselves, and who spend charitably out of what We have given them" (42:38).

This verse teaches Muslims the principle of democracy ("counsel among themselves") for conducting state affairs, and at the same time urges them to acquire the qualities that spiritualize man and draw him closer to God. Islam thus requires temporal authority to be exercised with the fullest sense of responsibility towards the Higher Divine Authority, making the physical force of the state subject to moral considerations. Hence it is that, according to Islamic teachings, the government is to be entrusted to persons who stand on a very high moral and spiritual plane, the head of state being called both an *amīr* (lit. one who commands) and an *imām* (a person whose high moral example is followed).

The principles of Islamic government were illustrated in practice by the Holy Prophet Muhammad himself as founder-head of the Muslim state; and after him, his first four successors are recognized as following in his footsteps to exemplify true Islamic rule, combining democracy with a display of high moral character. This model Islamic state was democratic in the truest sense of the word. Each of these successors ("Caliphs") was elected head of state by the agreement of all parties. The head was a servant of the state who was paid a fixed salary out of the public treasury, like all other public servants. He had no special privileges. Even the Holy Prophet himself did not claim any rights beyond those which other Muslims had. It was a democracy free from all differences of heredity, rank or privilege. All people, including the ruler, had equal rights and obligations and were subject to the same law.

Those entrusted with the work of government were required to work for the good of the people, to lead simple lives and to be easily accessible to the public, to provide for those who could not earn, and to have as much regard for the rights of non-Muslims as for those of the Muslims. The people's responsibility to the state is to respect and obey its laws as long as they do not involve disobedience to God and His Messenger. Abu Bakr, the first successor to the Holy Prophet, said in his very first address:

> "Help me if I am in the right, and correct me if I am in the wrong. Obey me as long as I obey God and His Messenger. In case I disobey them, I have no right to obedience from you."

People were thus also required to "correct" the authorities when necessary. "One of the most meritorious deeds," observed the Holy Prophet, "is to address a word of remonstrance to an unjust ruler".

Some illustrations of true Islamic rule

The Caliphate of Umar (d. 644 C.E.), during whose rule the Muslim dominion covered the vast territory of Arabia, Iraq, Iran, Palestine and Egypt, provides a great many examples of true Islamic democracy and rule in action. During his time, there were two consultative bodies: a general assembly in which affairs of special national importance were discussed, and a smaller committee for the conduct of daily business. Non-Muslims were also invited to take part in these consultations. As a rule, provincial governors were appointed after consulting the local population. In case of a complaint against a governor by the public, the governor was dismissed if found guilty. Pledges were taken from high state officials that they would not wear fine clothes, that they would ever keep their doors open to the needy, and that they would never keep guards at their doors.

Every individual citizen of the state of Islam, Muslim or non-Muslim, enjoyed the right to give his (or her) opinion and was perfectly free to do so. Once when Umar was delivering a sermon, it was a woman who stood up and objected to it. Far from resenting this, Umar accepted her criticism and acknowledged his error in the words: "The women of this city have more understanding than Umar". The position of the head of state was exactly that of a common subject. Once, when sued, Umar appeared to defend himself in court just as any other defendant. Thus under Umar the principle of democracy was carried to a point to which even the modern world has not yet attained. [1]

Jihad

There exists a great misconception regarding *jihād* (lit. *striving* or *struggle*), one of the religious obligations of a Muslim. In the terminology of Islam, *jihād* is applied both to the purely missionary activities of a Muslim and to his defence of the faith in a physical sense. The first duty, the duty to invite people to Islam, is a permanent duty laid upon all Muslims of all times, while the second is a duty which arises upon certain contingencies. According to the Quran, a jihad which it calls *jihād-an kabīr-an,* or the great jihad, must be carried on against the unbelievers *by means of the Holy Book itself* (see 25:52). Islam's greatest jihad is, therefore, not by means of the sword but by means of the Quran, i.e., a missionary effort to carry the message of Islam to all nations. Compulsion in religion is forbidden in clear words: "There is no compulsion in religion" (2:256). And there is not a single instance in the Holy Prophet's life in which an individual was ever required to confess the faith of Islam at the point of the sword.

As regards war and fighting, it is allowed only as a defensive measure against those who take up the sword to annihilate Islam:

"Permission to fight is granted to those upon whom war is made, because they are oppressed" (22:39).
"Fight in the way of God with those who fight with you, and do not exceed this limit" (2:190).

This does not leave the slightest doubt that Islam does not allow aggressive war, nor war for expansion or prestige. It only allows war when a state has been attacked. And even then, if the enemy offers peace, peace must be concluded:

"If they incline to peace, you should also incline to it, and trust in God" (8:39).

All the battles fought by the Holy Prophet Muhammad and the early

---

1. It may be noted that this inspiring display of the high ideals of Islam came about not due to the introduction of a set of formal laws (or the "enforcement of the Islamic system", as runs the modern political slogan), but because of the inner, moral reform produced in his followers by the Holy Prophet Muhammad — *Publisher.*

Muslims were purely defensive. He and his followers had been subjected to the severest persecution, as Islam began to gain ground at Makka. Even when they fled from their homes and took refuge in distant Madina, the powerful warriors of Makka attacked them in their new homes. Three times did the enemy attack Madina with strong forces to annihilate the Muslim community there. The Quran, therefore, allowed fighting only to save a persecuted community from powerful oppressors.

The Holy Prophet was peace-loving by nature, and he believed that making a generous peace was often a better remedy for aggression than annihilation of the aggressor, because it may bring about a real change of heart in the enemy. Hence it was that when, at last, the time came to punish the brutal aggressors, who were at the mercy of the Holy Prophet at the Muslim conquest of Makka, he not only awarded them a general amnesty but let them off without even a reprimand. This act of generosity towards one's inveterate enemy stands unique in the annals of the world.

Zakāt and Charity

I shall note one more peculiarity of the brotherhood of Islam. Every religion of the world has preached charity, but it is in Islam only that it has been made obligatory and binding upon all those who accept the Muslim faith. Here we have a brotherhood into which the rich man cannot enter unless and until he is willing to give a part of his possessions for the poorer members of the brotherhood. There is no doubt that the rich man is not here confronted with the insuperable difficulty of the ideal test of the camel passing through the eye of the needle, but he is subjected to a practical test which not only makes him stand on the same footing with his poorest brother, but also requires him to pay a tax, known as *Zakāt*, a tax which is levied on the rich for the benefit of the poor.

Everyone who possesses property above a certain limit is required to set apart a stated portion thereof. The portion so set apart should be collected by the Muslim state, or the Muslim community when there is no Muslim state, and the objects to which it must be devoted are enumerated in the following verse:

"*Zakāt* is only for the poor and the needy, and those employed to administer it, and those whose hearts are made to incline to truth, and to free the captives, and (to help) those in debt, and in the way of God, and for the wayfarer" (9:60).

The words *way of God* include every charitable purpose. *Zakāt* stands unique both as charity and as tax. As charity it is obligatory, but the obligation is moral. As tax, the sanction behind it is moral, not the physical force of a state. *Zakāt*, therefore, acts not only as a levelling influence but also as a means of developing the higher sentiments of man—the sentiments of love and sympathy towards his fellow-man. It should be noted that, according to the Quran, a charitable deed must be done as a duty which man owes to man, so that it conveys no idea of superiority of the giver or inferiority of the receiver (see 2:262-264).

Besides the contributions the payment of which has thus been made obligatory by the Holy Quran and made as compulsory as the saying of prayers, general charity is inculcated very forcibly throughout the Holy Book. It not only lays stress on such great deeds of charity as the emancipation of slaves (2:177, 90:13), the feeding of the poor (69:34, etc.), taking care of the orphans (17:34, etc.), and doing good to humanity in general, but gives equal prominence to smaller acts of benevolence the withholding of which is stated to be against the spirit of prayer (107:4-7).

In the Holy Prophet's Sayings, charity is given the broadest possible significance. "To remove from the road anything which may cause harm", or "to show someone the way", or even to give food to one's family or oneself, are charitable deeds. The doing of good to the dumb creation is also called charity: "Whoever tills a field, and birds and beasts eat of it, it is charity". The Holy Quran also speaks of extending charity not only to all men including believers and unbelievers (2:272), but also to the dumb creation (51:19).

Charity must be given out of good things, out of things which a man loves for himself:

"O you who believe! Give in charity out of the good things that you earn . . . and do not aim at giving in charity that which is bad, while you would not take it for yourself" (2:267).

Love of God should be the motive in all charitable deeds:

> "(The righteous) give food, out of love for Him, to the poor and the orphan and the captive, saying, We feed you for God's pleasure only - we desire from you neither reward nor thanks" (76:8,9).

11. SCOPE OF MORAL TEACHINGS

The Holy Quran was not meant for one people or one age, and accordingly the scope of its moral teachings is as wide as humanity itself. It is a Book which offers guidance to all men in all conditions of life, to the ignorant savage as well as to the wise philosopher, to the man of business as well as to the recluse, to the rich as well as to the poor. Accordingly, while giving varied rules of life, it appeals to the individual to follow the best rules which are applicable to the circumstances under which he lives (39:55). If it contains directions on the one hand which are calculated to raise men in the lowest grades of civilization and to teach them the crude manners of society, it also furnishes rules of guidance to men in the highest stages of moral and spiritual progress. High ideal moral teachings are no doubt necessary to the progress of man, but only those who can realize those ideals will be able to benefit by them. But to this class do not belong the vast masses in any nation or community, however high may be its standard of civilization. Hence the Quran contains rules of guidance for all the stages through which man has to pass in the onward march from the condition of the savage to that of the highly spiritual man. They cover all the branches of human activity and require the development of all the faculties of man.

Islam requires the display of every quality that has been placed in man, and makes only one limitation, viz., that it should be displayed on the proper occasion. It requires a man to show meekness as well as courage, but each on its proper occasion. It teaches forgiveness, but at the same time it requires that when the nature of an offence requires punishment, punishment proportionate to the crime must be administered. It says, "Forgive when you see that forgiveness would be conducive to good." Again, it teaches men to display high morals under the most adverse circumstances, to be honest even when honesty is likely to lead one into complications, to speak truth even when one's truthful statement is against those nearest and dearest to one, to show sympathy even at the sacrifice of one's own interest, to be patient under the hardest afflictions, to be good even to those who have done evil. At the same time it teaches the middle path; it teaches men to exercise the noble qualities which have been placed in their nature by God while transacting their own affairs. It does not inculcate severance from one's worldly connections; it requires them to serve God, but not as monks; it enjoins them to spend their wealth, but not in such a manner as to sit down "blamed and straitened in means"; it teaches them to be submissive, but not by losing self-respect; it exhorts them to forgive, but not in such a manner as to embolden culprits; it allows them to exercise all their rights, but not so as to violate others'; and last of all, it requires them to preach their own religion, but not by abusing others.